NEW LOOK

Inside and Outside

Henry Pluckrose
Photography by Steve Shott

Watts Books
London • New York • Sydney

Let us start with a thought.
Every outside has an inside.

Every container –
a bottle, a jar, a box –
has an inside
and an outside.

The colour, shape, and size of a container help us to guess what is stored inside. You would not find breakfast cereal in a teapot...

jam in a milk jug — or tea in a bowl.

However, things which look similar from the outside ...

might not contain what you expect on the inside!

Sometimes a box might contain a big surprise!

You would not
expect to find
an elephant inside a pencil tin!

Peel a banana or an orange —

or bite into an apple. Is the outside different from the inside?

Outsides need insides.
Without an inside,
where would we put our legs?

Inside can mean a place where things are kept safe. Eggs are safe inside a nest.

Chicks grow safely inside an egg.

This is the outside of a building.

What might you find inside?

Were you right?

what the outside might look like.
Can you match inside to outside?

Sometimes we can be inside and look outside ...

or be outside and look inside …

and even be inside and look inside.

A rabbit might be outside and look outside.

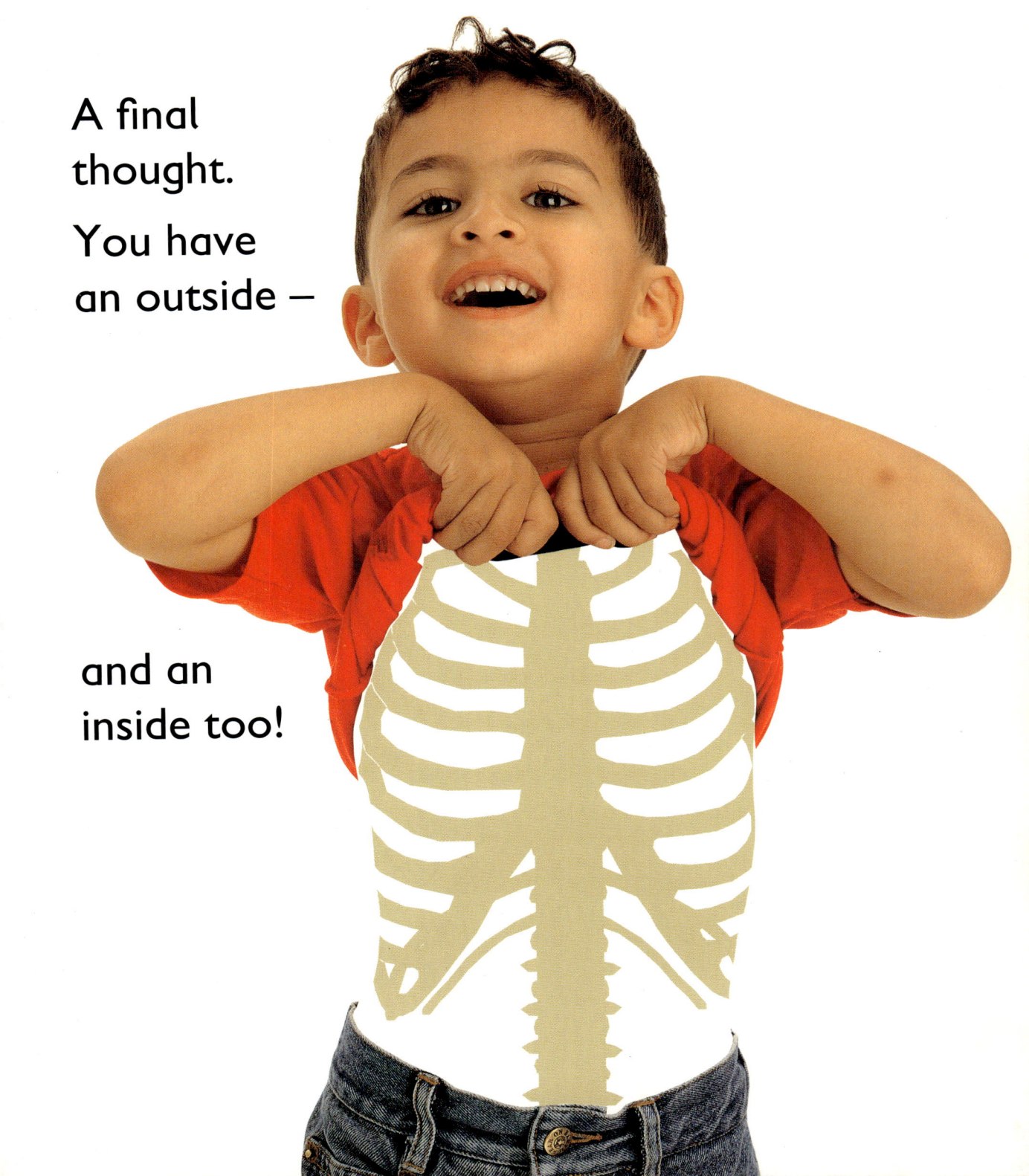

A final thought.

You have an outside —

and an inside too!

About this book

This book has been prepared for use in the home, playgroup, nursery and infant school.

The world in which young children grow and develop is a fascinating place. New experiences – things tasted, touched, heard, smelt and seen – crowd one upon another. Such experiences are the key to understanding, for their very richness and diversity fosters curiosity and encourages questioning.

We express our discoveries, our ideas and our thoughts through words. Without language, thoughts could not be shared or ideas deepened and clarified. This marriage of words with first hand experience is one of the keys to intellectual development.

Children view the world from a different eye level to adults and spend their formative years in an environment specifically created for adults. This book, along with its companions in the series, is a visual exploration of everyday life from the child's viewpoint. The photographs and the text encourage talk and personal discovery – both vital elements in the learning process.

Henry Pluckrose

About the author

Henry Pluckrose is a very well known educationalist and respected author of many information books for young people. He is a former primary school headmaster who is now an educational consultant for different organisations at home and abroad.

Additional photographs:
Mike Davis 17 (bottom);
Robert Harding Picture Library 17 (top)

Animals supplied by:
Trevor Smith's Animal World

© 1995 Watts Books

Watts Books
96 Leonard Street
London EC2A 4RH

Franklin Watts Australia
14 Mars Road
Lane Cove
NSW 2066

UK ISBN: 0 7496 1891 4

10 9 8 7 6 5 4 3 2 1

Editor: Annabel Martin
Design: Mike Davis

A CIP catalogue record for this book is available from the British Library

Dewey Decimal Classification: 600

Printed in Malaysia